This book belongs to:

_____

_____

This book is designed to encourage small children to talk about what they see in the colorful pictures. Some simple questions have been suggested, but many more can be made up.

Always try to find a quiet space to share this book with your child. Children will be generous with their responses if you encourage them and give them confidence. They learn new words quickly and love to use them. A good vocabulary helps them think and enables them to express their thoughts.

Most important, enjoy the book together.

Written by Kath Jewitt
Illustrated by Claire Henley
Language consultant: Betty Root

This is a Parragon Publishing book
First published in 2005

Parragon Publishing
Queen Street House
4 Queen Street
Bath, BA1 1HE, UK
Copyright © Parragon 2005

ISBN 1-40544-559-9
Printed in China

My First Book of...

FARM ANIMALS

COCK-A-DOODLE-DO!

The rooster wakes the farm animals every morning.

Point to the farm animals in the picture.

All these different animals live on the farm.

sheep

hen

horse

cat

rooster

Look at each animal and say its name.

goat

cow

dog

pig

duck

The farmer feeds the animals every morning.

What are these animals having for breakfast?

Each farm animal lives in one of these houses.

henhouse

kennel

This naughty animal is eating the farmer's laundry!

Do you know what the animal is called? Can you point to another goat in the picture?

Pigs have short, curly tails.

Look at these tails and
say who they belong to.

Do you know what noise these farm animals make?

cluck!

baa!

neigh!

oink!

There are lots of baby animals in this picture.

calf

chicks

lamb

puppy

Say each one's name out loud.

kid

foal

piglet

ducklings

This is a baby sheep.
It is called a lamb.

Find the lamb's mommy.

What is the farmer doing?

Cows give us fresh milk.

Which of these animals gives us wool?

Hens lay eggs.
How many hens can you see?

The farmer is collecting an egg for his breakfast. Do you like eggs for your breakfast, too?

Can you point to the animal that doesn't belong on the farm?

Which animal is your favorite?